SELECTED BAB BALLADS

SELECTED

BAB BALLADS

WRITTEN AND ILLUSTRATED BY

W. S. GILBERT

WITH AN INTRODUCTION BY

HESKETH PEARSON

AND A NOTE ON GILBERT AS ILLUSTRATOR BY

PHILIP JAMES

CHRISTMAS 1955

MADE AND PRINTED IN GREAT BRITAIN

Contents

Introduction 7

SELECTED BAB BALLADS

Captain Reece 17
The Rival Curates 23
The Bishop and the 'Busman 29
Babette's Love 34
The Yarn of the 'Nancy Bell' 39
The Bishop of Rum-ti-Foo 44
Baines Carew, Gentleman 50
Thomas Winterbottom Hance 56
A Discontented Sugar Broker 62
Ellen McJones Aberdeen 68
Gentle Alice Brown 73
Annie Protheroe 78
Gregory Parable, LL.D. 84
The Modest Couple 90
Emily, John, James, and I 96
Hongree and Mahry 101
Etiquette 107

APPENDIX

A Note on Gilbert as Illustrator 117
Collotype Plates 121

Note

THE illustrations of 'The Bishop and the 'Busman', 'Babette's Love', 'The Yarn of the "Nancy Bell" ', 'Gregory Parable, LL.D.', and 'The Modest Couple' are reproduced from the line-engravings in *The Bab Ballads*, 1898. All others are reproduced from the original wood-engravings, and their text does not incorporate the changes made by the author for the 1898 edition of the *Ballads*. In the collotype appendix, some of Gilbert's illustrations engraved on wood by the Dalziels for the original editions are shown with his pencil sketches and his final drawings for the 1898 edition. The sketches are reproduced from Gilbert's unpublished sketch-books by kind permission of the Executor of Miss Nancy McIntosh, and the final drawings from the originals in the British Museum.

Introduction

BY HESKETH PEARSON

As a child Gilbert was called BAB by his family, and so we may say that with this abbreviation his parents christened *The Bab Ballads*, which were written for grown-up babies, a description that fits the greater part of the human race. Gilbert completed his education at King's College, London, and his first printed verses appeared in the college magazine; but they did not foreshadow the future balladist, who was a demon for work and acquired by constant practice and steady labour his ultimate dexterity. No man ever made greater efforts to open the tenuous vein of genius within him. With the sole intention of becoming rich and famous, he toiled at his prose and polished his verses, exhausting much oil and many candles during the hours he could spare from earning a living, first as an unhappy government clerk and next as an unfortunate barrister. It seems that writers of light verse cannot resist the law, for not only Gilbert but W. M. Praed, C. S. Calverley, and H. J. Byron were barristers. The last-named started Gilbert on his literary career.

In 1861 a competitor to *Punch* was launched, and in the hope that it would surpass that periodical in one respect the founders called it *Fun*. The first editor was H. J. Byron, who lived to write the most successful farce of his age, *Our Boys*, which ran for over four years at the Vaudeville Theatre, but whose chief claim to our attention is that he promptly spotted Gilbert's peculiar quality as a writer. 'With much labour I turned out an article three-quarters of a column long, and sent it to the editor, together with a half-page drawing on wood.' Such is Gilbert's own account. He had drudged at drawing as conscientiously as he had at writing, teaching himself as he went along. The effect produced on the editor by that illustrated article staggered the young author. Byron sent a member of his staff to call on Gilbert with the request that he should contribute a column of letterpress and a half-page drawing every week for the rest of his life. 'But that little thing I sent you the other day is all I can do,' objected Gilbert, who was under the impression that he had put everything into his first essay, that he had emptied himself of knowledge and exhausted his means of expression. But he was persuaded to have another shot, with the result that he continued to fire off articles and verses at the same target for the next ten years.

Nothing has survived from that barrage of prose and rhyme except *The Bab Ballads*, which exist in their own right and also as the source of many ditties and ideas in the Savoy operas. Lots of the ballads, Gilbert confessed, 'were composed hastily, and under the discomforting necessity of having to turn out a quantity of lively verse on a certain day in each week'. One of them was actually composed in the train to Folkestone on his honeymoon. His diligence was quickly rewarded, the ballads being quoted on the Stock Exchange. Men who cared solely for facts and nothing for rhymes enjoyed the fancies and jingles of BAB, which soon became the favourite literature of sailors, soldiers, doctors, lawyers, bankers, stockbrokers, and other unpoetical persons. The ballads were heard at smoking concerts, at club dinners, at all sorts of Bohemian gatherings. They were a godsend to actors, whose recitation of a BAB ensured laughter and applause. They arrived at a moment perfectly suited to their themes and treatment. Dickens had just produced *Our Mutual Friend*. Wilkie Collins was writing *The Moonstone*. It was a period when a mixture of broad comedy and bloodshed, humour and horror, pleased the palate of the reading public; and such ingredients, made fantastic by grave exaggeration and ridiculous by combination, gave the ballads an instantaneous popularity.

A first instalment of *The Bab Ballads* was published in 1869, being followed by *More Bab Ballads* in 1873. They sold like hot cakes, and a selection of

Fifty Bab Ballads came out in 1877, the persistent demand necessitating a collected edition, to which were added a number of popular songs from the Savoy operas, in 1898. For this final version, often reprinted, Gilbert made a number of new drawings, explaining that the original illustrations 'erred gravely in the direction of unnecessary extravagance'. But the true explanation was that the Gilbert of 1898 had become a different man from the BAB of thirty years earlier. BAB had enjoyed fun for fun's sake. The Gilbert of the operas had become a satirist.

Some writers have detected a streak of cruelty in *The Bab Ballads*; but it was merely the full-blooded jocularity of a man whose energy was bursting for expression. All writing is in a sense autobiographical, for it contains the seed of the extravert's nature, the flower of the introvert's. Gilbert was the former, and we could surmise from the ballads that he was a somewhat ruthless, very high-spirited, and occasionally violent fellow, whose desire for domination took the form of fanciful and comical brutality.

His temper has been classified
As hasty; but he's very quickly pacified,

he wrote of himself in one of his ballads, and it may further be claimed that his fictional cruelty reflected the baffled nature of a man of action, not the free nature of the artist. It was the ferocity of a man who would not harm a fly. He could cut people to bits in rhyme but would have tended a hurt insect in reality. 'I have a constitutional objection to taking life in any form,' he once said. 'I don't think I ever wittingly killed a black-beetle . . . the mechanism of life is so wonderful that I shrink from stopping its action.' Fanciful savagery is also the obverse of whimsical sentimentality, and anyone who has read some of Gilbert's plays will turn with relief to the farcical tortures of BAB.

The curious thing is that some of the ballads were a little too indelicate even for the rough-and-tumble eighteen-sixties. Gilbert sent 'The Yarn of the "Nancy Bell"' to *Punch*, which had already published some of his stuff, and the editor, Mark Lemon, rejected it as too cannibalistic for the taste of his readers. Gilbert thereupon ceased his connexion with *Punch*, and took his revenge on the next editor, Burnand. 'Do you ever receive good jokes and things from outsiders?' someone mildly inquired. 'Oh, often!' said Burnand. 'They never appear,' Gilbert grunted.

Though he could feel affronted by an editor's rejection, BAB had a low opinion of his ballads. 'I have ventured to publish the little pictures with them,' he noted in the first edition, 'because, while they are certainly quite as bad as the ballads, I suppose they are not much worse.' His attitude was due to a growing feeling that he was made for better things. 'I can do something more than wear the cap and bells,' he declared. The 'something more' consisted of a series of plays, several in verse, which he regarded as his highest achievement, assuring his first biographer that 'rightly or wrongly, in the pre-Savoy days I held the foremost position among dramatic authors', and referring to 'the easy trivialities of the Savoy *libretti*'. Gilbert was in fact the born clown who longed to play Hamlet. His plays are unrevivable and almost unreadable; but BAB remains a joy, and it is difficult to make a selection from the ballads because nearly everyone who likes them likes nearly every one of them.

When Gilbert wrote them he was merely letting off steam, larking for the sake of the lark. He had not yet seen himself as a reformer. He could enjoy standing things upside down for the mere amusement of seeing them in that position. Later he became a satirist, a critic of life, one of whose objects in standing things upside down was to get them right side up. If we compare 'The Rival Curates' of BAB with the rival poets of *Patience*, we see the difference between a pure joke and a social satire. Nevertheless there is an implied punch behind Gilbert's playfulness. His humour is not that of parody or nonsense, like the verses of Lewis Carroll and Edward Lear. BAB represents the view that life is radically ridiculous, a view shared by every healthy and intelligent person at rare moments of revelation. The reason we still delight in the ballads is that theirs is the art of unalloyed absurdity, which will never become out of date unless the world and its inhabitants are totally transformed or totalitarianly standardized.

SELECTED BAB BALLADS

Captain Reece

OF all the ships upon the blue,
No ship contained a better crew
Than that of worthy CAPTAIN REECE,
Commanding of *The Mantelpiece.*

He was adored by all his men,
For worthy CAPTAIN REECE, R.N.,
Did all that lay within him to
Promote the comfort of his crew.

If ever they were dull or sad,
Their captain danced to them like mad,
Or told, to make the time pass by,
Droll legends of his infancy.

A feather bed had every man,
Warm slippers and hot-water can,
Brown windsor from the captain's store,
A valet, too, to every four.

Did they with thirst in summer burn,
Lo, seltzogenes at every turn,
And on all very sultry days
Cream ices handed round on trays.

Then currant wine and ginger pops
Stood handily on all the 'tops';
And, also, with amusement rife,
A 'Zoetrope, or Wheel of Life'.

New volumes came across the sea
From MISTER MUDIE's libraree;
The Times and *Saturday Review*
Beguiled the leisure of the crew.

Kind-hearted CAPTAIN REECE, R.N.,
Was quite devoted to his men;
In point of fact, good CAPTAIN REECE
Beatified *The Mantelpiece.*

One summer eve, at half-past ten,
He said (addressing all his men):
'Come, tell me, please, what I can do
To please and gratify my crew.

'By any reasonable plan
I'll make you happy if I can;
My own convenience count as *nil*;
It is my duty, and I will.'

Then up and answered WILLIAM LEE
(The kindly captain's coxswain he,
A nervous, shy, low-spoken man),
He cleared his throat and thus began:

'You have a daughter, Captain Reece,
Ten female cousins and a niece,
A ma, if what I'm told is true,
Six sisters, and an aunt or two.

'Now, somehow, sir, it seems to me,
More friendly-like we all should be
If you united of 'em to
Unmarried members of the crew.

'If you'd ameliorate our life,
Let each select from them a wife;
And as for nervous me, old pal,
Give me your own enchanting gal!'

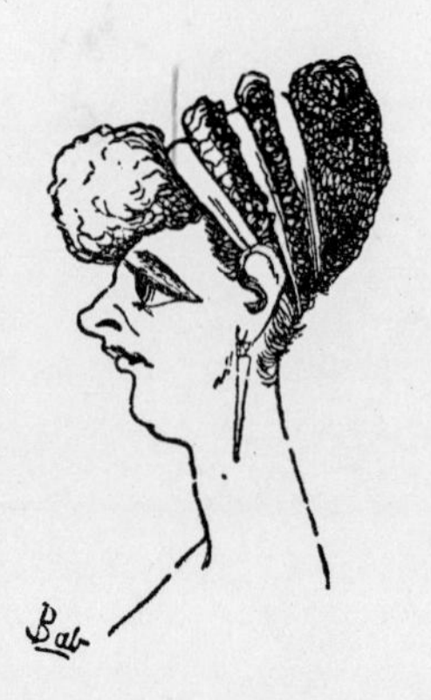

Good Captain Reece, that worthy man,
Debated on his coxswain's plan:
'I quite agree,' he said, 'O Bill;
It is my duty, and I will.

'My daughter, that enchanting gurl,
Has just been promised to an Earl,
And all my other familee,
To peers of various degree.

'But what are dukes and viscounts to
The happiness of all my crew?
The word I gave you I'll fulfil;
It is my duty, and I will.

'As you desire it shall befall,
I'll settle thousands on you all,
And I shall be, despite my hoard,
The only bachelor on board.'

The boatswain of *The Mantelpiece*,
He blushed and spoke to CAPTAIN REECE:
'I beg your honour's leave,' he said;
'If you would wish to go and wed,

'I have a widowed mother who
Would be the very thing for you –
She long has loved you from afar,
She washes for you, CAPTAIN R.'

The Captain saw the dame that day –
Addressed her in his playful way –
'And did it want a wedding ring?
It was a tempting ickle sing!

'Well, well, the chaplain I will seek,
We'll all be married this day week
At yonder church upon the hill;
It is my duty, and I will!'

The sisters, cousins, aunts, and niece,
And widowed Ma of CAPTAIN REECE,
Attended there as they were bid;
It was their duty, and they did.

The Rival Curates

LIST while the poet trolls
  Of MR CLAYTON HOOPER,
Who had a cure of souls
  At Spiffton-extra-Sooper.

He lived on curds and whey,
  And daily sang their praises,
And then he'd go and play
  With buttercups and daisies.

Wild croquet HOOPER banned,
  And all the sports of Mammon,
He warred with cribbage, and
  He exorcized backgammon.

His helmet was a glance
  That spoke of holy gladness;
A saintly smile his lance;
  His shield a tear of sadness.

His Vicar smiled to see
  This armour on him buckled;
With pardonable glee
  He blessed himself and chuckled.

'In mildness to abound
My curate's sole design is;
In all the country round
There's none so mild as mine is!'

And HOOPER, disinclined
His trumpet to be blowing,
Yet didn't think you'd find
A milder curate going.

A friend arrived one day
At Spiffton-extra-Sooper,
And in this shameful way
He spoke to MR HOOPER:

'You think your famous name
For mildness can't be shaken,
That none can blot your fame –
But, HOOPER, you're mistaken!

'Your mind is not as blank
As that of Hopley Porter,
Who holds a curate's rank
At Assesmilk-cum-Worter.

'*He* plays the airy flute,
And looks depressed and blighted,
Doves round about him «toot»,
And lambkins dance delighted.

'*He* labours more than you
At worsted work, and frames it;
In old maids' albums, too,
Sticks seaweed – yes, and names it!'

The tempter said his say,
Which pierced him like a needle –
He summoned straight away
His sexton and his beadle.

(These men were men who could
  Hold liberal opinions:
On Sundays they were good –
  On week-days they were minions.)

'To HOPLEY PORTER go,
  Your fare I will afford you –
Deal him a deadly blow,
  And blessings shall reward you.

'But stay – I do not like
  Undue assassination,
And so, before you strike,
  Make this communication:

'I'll give him this one chance –
  If he'll more gaily bear him,
Play croquet, smoke, and dance,
  I willingly will spare him.'

They went, those minions true,
  To Assesmilk-cum-Worter,
And told their errand to
  The REVEREND HOPLEY PORTER.

'What?' said that reverend gent,
  'Dance through my hours of leisure?
Smoke? – bathe myself with scent? –
  Play croquet? Oh, with pleasure!

'Wear all my hair in curl?
  Stand at my door, and wink – so –
At every passing girl?
  My brothers, I should think so!

'For years I've longed for some
Excuse for this revulsion:
Now that excuse has come –
I do it on compulsion!!!'

He smoked and winked away –
This REVEREND HOPLEY PORTER –
The deuce there was to pay
At Assesmilk-cum-Worter.

And HOOPER holds his ground,
In mildness daily growing –
They think him, all around,
The mildest curate going.

The Bishop and the 'Busman

IT was a Bishop bold,
  And London was his see,
He was short and stout and round about
  And zealous as could be.

It also was a Jew,
  Who drove a Putney 'bus –
For flesh of swine however fine
  He did not care a cuss.

His name was HASH BAZ BEN,
  And JEDEDIAH too,
And SOLOMON and ZABULON –
  This 'bus-directing Jew.

The Bishop said, said he,
  'I'll see what I can do
To Christianize and make you wise,
  You poor benighted Jew.'

So every blessed day
  That 'bus he rode outside,
From Fulham town, both up and down,
  And loudly thus he cried:

'His name is HASH BAZ BEN,
  And JEDEDIAH too,
And SOLOMON and ZABULON –
  This 'bus-directing Jew.'

At first the 'busman smiled,
  And rather liked the fun –
He merely smiled, that Hebrew child,
  And said, 'Eccentric one!'

And gay young dogs would wait
  To see the 'bus go by
(These gay young dogs, in striking togs),
  To hear the Bishop cry:

'Observe his grisly beard,
  His race it clearly shows,
He sticks no fork in ham or pork –
  Observe, my friends, his nose.

'His name is HASH BAZ BEN,
   And JEDEDIAH too,
And SOLOMON and ZABULON –
   This 'bus-directing Jew.'

But though at first amused,
   Yet after seven years,
This Hebrew child got rather riled,
   And melted into tears.

He really almost feared
   To leave his poor abode,
His nose, and name, and beard became
   A byword on that road.

At length he swore an oath,
The reason he would know –
'I'll call and see why ever he
Does persecute me so!'

The good old Bishop sat
On his ancestral chair,
The 'busman came, sent up his name,
And laid his grievance bare.

'Benighted Jew,' he said
(The good old Bishop did),
'Be Christian, you, instead of Jew –
Become a Christian kid!

'I'll ne'er annoy you more.'
'Indeed?' replied the Jew;
'Shall I be freed?' 'You will, indeed!'
Then 'Done!' said he, 'with you!'

The organ which, in man,
  Between the eyebrows grows,
Fell from his face, and in its place
  He found a Christian nose.

His tangled Hebrew beard,
  Which to his waist came down,
Was now a pair of whiskers fair –
  His name ADOLPHUS BROWN!

He wedded in a year
  That prelate's daughter JANE,
He's grown quite fair – has auburn hair –
  His wife is far from plain.

Babette's Love

BABETTE she was a fisher gal,
With jupon striped and cap in crimps.
She passed her days inside the Halle,
Or catching little nimble shrimps.
Yet she was sweet as flowers in May,
With no professional bouquet.

JACOT was, of the Customs bold,
An officer, at gay Boulogne,
He loved BABETTE – his love he told,
And sighed, 'Oh, soyez vous my own!'
But 'Non!' said she, 'JACOT, my pet,
Vous êtes trop scraggy pour BABETTE.

‘Of one alone I nightly dream,
An able mariner is he,
And gaily serves the Gen’ral Steam-
Boat Navigation Companee.
I’ll marry him, if he but will –
His name, I rather think, is Bill.

‘I see him when he’s not aware,
Upon our hospitable coast,
Reclining with an easy air
Upon the *Port* against a post,
A-thinking of, I’ll dare to say,
His native Chelsea far away!’

‘Oh, mon!’ exclaimed the Customs bold,
‘Mes yeux!’ he said (which means ‘my eye’).
‘Oh, chère!’ he also cried, I’m told,
‘Par Jove,’ he added, with a sigh.

'Oh, mon! oh, chère! mes yeux! par Jove!
Je n'aime pas cet enticing cove!'

The *Panther's* captain stood hard by,
He was a man of morals strict,
If e'er a sailor winked his eye,
Straightway he had that sailor licked,
Mast-headed all (such was his code)
Who dashed or jiggered, blessed or blowed.

He wept to think a tar of his
Should lean so gracefully on posts,
He sighed and sobbed to think of this,
On foreign, French, and friendly coasts.
'It's human natur', p'raps – if so,
Oh, isn't human natur' low!'

He called his BILL, who pulled his curl,
He said, 'My BILL, I understand
You've captivated some young gurl
On this here French and foreign land.
Her tender heart your beauties jog –
They do, you know they do, you dog.

'You have a graceful way I learn
Of leaning airily on posts,
By which you've been and caused to burn
A tender flame on these here coasts.
A fisher gurl, I much regret, –
Her age, sixteen – her name, BABETTE.

'You'll marry her, you gentle tar –
  Your union I myself will bless,
And when you matrimonied are,
  I will appoint her stewardess.'
But WILLIAM hitched himself and sighed,
And cleared his throat, and thus replied:

'Not so: unless you're fond of strife,
  You'd better mind your own affairs,
I have an able-bodied wife
  Awaiting me at Wapping Stairs;
If all this here to her I tell,
She'll larrup you and me as well.

'Skin-deep, and valued at a pin,
  Is beauty such as VENUS owns –
Her beauty is beneath her skin,
  And lies in layers on her bones.

The other sailors of the crew
They always calls her «Whopping Sue!»'

'Oho!' the Captain said, 'I see!
And is she then so very strong?'
'She'd take your honour's scruff,' said he,
  'And pitch you over to Bolong!'
'I pardon you,' the Captain said,
'The fair BABETTE you needn't wed.'

Perhaps the Customs had his will,
  And coaxed the scornful girl to wed,
Perhaps the Captain and his BILL,
  And WILLIAM's little wife are dead;
Or p'raps they're all alive and well:
I cannot, cannot, cannot tell.

The Yarn of the 'Nancy Bell'

'TWAS on the shores that round our coast
From Deal to Ramsgate span,
That I found alone on a piece of stone
An elderly naval man.

His hair was weedy, his beard was long,
And weedy and long was he,
And I heard this wight on the shore recite,
In a singular minor key:

'Oh, I am a cook and a captain bold,
And the mate of the *Nancy* brig,
And a bo'sun tight, and a midshipmite,
And the crew of the captain's gig.'

And he shook his fists and he tore his hair,
Till I really felt afraid,
For I couldn't help thinking the man had been drinking,
And so I simply said:

'Oh, elderly man, it's little I know
Of the duties of men of the sea,
But I'll eat my hand if I understand
How you can possibly be

'At once a cook, and a captain bold,
And the mate of the *Nancy* brig,
And a bo'sun tight, and a midshipmite,
And the crew of the captain's gig.'

Then he gave a hitch to his trousers, which
Is a trick all seamen larn,
And having got rid of a thumping quid,
He spun this painful yarn:

''Twas in the good ship *Nancy Bell*
That we sailed to the Indian sea,
And there on a reef we come to grief,
Which has often occurred to me.

'And pretty nigh all o' the crew was drowned
(There was seventy-seven o' soul),
And only ten of the *Nancy's* men
Said «Here!» to the muster-roll.

'There was me and the cook and the captain bold,
And the mate of the *Nancy* brig,
And the bo'sun tight, and a midshipmite,
And the crew of the captain's gig.

'For a month we'd neither wittles nor drink,
Till a-hungry we did feel,
So we drawed a lot, and accordin' shot
The captain for our meal.

'The next lot fell to the *Nancy's* mate,
And a delicate dish he made;
Then our appetite with the midshipmite
We seven survivors stayed.

'And then we murdered the bo'sun tight,
And he much resembled pig;
Then we wittled free, did the cook and me,
On the crew of the captain's gig.

'Then only the cook and me was left,
And the delicate question, «Which
Of us two goes to the kettle?» arose,
And we argued it out as sich.

'For I loved that cook as a brother, I did,
And the cook he worshipped me;
But we'd both be blowed if we'd either be stowed
In the other chap's hold, you see.

'«I'll be eat if you dines off me,» says Tom,
«Yes, that,» says I, «you'll be,» –
«I'm boiled if I die, my friend,» quoth I,
And «Exactly so,» quoth he.

'Says he, «Dear James, to murder me
Were a foolish thing to do,
For don't you see that you can't cook *me*,
While I can – and will – cook *you!*»

'So he boils the water, and takes the salt
And the pepper in proportions true
(Which he never forgot), and some chopped shalot,
And some sage and parsley too.

'«Come here,» says he, with a proper pride,
Which his smiling features tell,
«'Twill soothing be if I let you see,
How extremely nice you'll smell.»

'And he stirred it round and round and round,
And he sniffed at the foaming broth;
When I ups with his heels, and smothers his squeals
In the scum of the boiling broth.

'And I eat that cook in a week or less,
And – as I eating be
The last of his chops, why, I almost drops,
For a wessel in sight I see!

* * * * *

'And I never grieve, and I never smile,
And I never larf nor play,
But I sit and croak, and a single joke
I have – which is to say:

'«Oh, I am a cook and a captain bold,
And the mate of the *Nancy* brig,
And a bo'sun tight, and a midshipmite,
And the crew of the captain's gig!»'

The Bishop of Rum-ti-Foo

FROM east and south the holy clan
Of Bishops gathered to a man;
To Synod, called Pan-Anglican,
    In flocking crowds they came.
Among them was a Bishop, who
Had lately been appointed to
The balmy isle of Rum-ti-Foo,
    And PETER was his name.

His people – twenty-three in sum –
They played the eloquent tum-tum,
And lived on scalps served up in rum –
    The only sauce they knew.
When first good Bishop PETER came
(For PETER was that Bishop's name),
To humour them, he did the same
    As they of Rum-ti-Foo.

His flock, I've often heard him tell,
(His name was PETER) loved him well,
And summoned by the sound of bell,
    In crowds together came.
'Oh, massa, why you go away?
Oh, MASSA PETER, please to stay.'
(They called him PETER, people say,
    Because it was his name.)

He told them all good boys to be,
And sailed away across the sea,
At London Bridge that Bishop he
    Arrived one Tuesday night;
And as that night he homeward strode
To his Pan-Anglican abode,
He passed along the Borough Road,
    And saw a gruesome sight.

He saw a crowd assembled round
A person dancing on the ground,
Who straight began to leap and bound
    With all his might and main.
To see that dancing man he stopped,
Who twirled and wriggled, skipped and hopped,
Then down incontinently dropped,
    And then sprang up again.

The Bishop chuckled at the sight,
'This style of dancing would delight
A simple Rum-ti-Foozleite.
I'll learn it if I can,
To please the tribe when I get back.'
He begged the man to teach his knack.
'Right Reverend Sir, in half a crack!'
Replied that dancing man.

The dancing man he worked away –
And taught the Bishop every day –
The dancer skipped like any fay –
Good PETER did the same.
The Bishop buckled to his task
With *battements*, cuts, and *pas de basque*
(I'll tell you, if you care to ask,
That PETER was his name).

'Come, walk like this,' the dancer said,
'Stick out your toes – stick in your head,
Stalk on with quick, galvanic tread –
Your fingers thus extend;
The attitude's considered quaint.'
The weary Bishop, feeling faint,
Replied, 'I do not say it ain't,
But «Time!» my Christian friend!'

'We now proceed to something new –
Dance as the PAYNES and LAURIS do,
Like this – one, two – one, two – one, two.'
The Bishop, never proud,
But in an overwhelming heat
(His name was PETER, I repeat)
Performed the PAYNE and LAURI feat,
And puffed his thanks aloud.

Another game the dancer planned –
'Just take your ankle in your hand,
And try, my lord, if you can stand –
Your body stiff and stark.
If, when revisiting your see,
You learnt to hop on shore – like me –
The novelty would striking be,
And must attract remark.'

'No,' said the worthy Bishop, 'No;
That is a length to which, I trow,
Colonial Bishops cannot go.
You may express surprise
At finding Bishops deal in pride –
But, if that trick I ever tried,
I should appear undignified
In Rum-ti-Foozle's eyes.

'The islanders of Rum-ti-Foo
Are well-conducted persons, who
Approve a joke as much as you,
And laugh at it as such;
But if they saw their Bishop land,
His leg supported in his hand,
The joke they wouldn't understand –
'Twould pain them very much!'

Baines Carew, Gentleman

Of all the good attorneys who
Have placed their names upon the roll,
But few could equal Baines Carew
For tender-heartedness and soul.

Whene'er he heard a tale of woe
From client A or client B,
His grief would overcome him so
He'd scarce have strength to take his fee.

It laid him up for many days,
When duty led him to distrain,
And serving writs, although it pays,
Gave him excruciating pain.

He made out costs, distrained for rent,
Foreclosed and sued, with moistened eye –
No bill of costs could represent
The value of such sympathy.

No charges can approximate
The worth of sympathy with woe; –
Although I think I ought to state
He did his best to make them so.

Of all the many clients who
Had mustered round his legal flag,
No single client of the crew
Was half so dear as CAPTAIN BAGG.

Now, CAPTAIN BAGG had bowed him to
A heavy matrimonial yoke –
His wifey had of faults a few –
She never could resist a joke.

Her chaff at first he meekly bore,
Till unendurable it grew.
'To stop this persecution sore
I will consult my friend CAREW.

'And when CAREW's advice I've got,
Divorce *a mensa* I shall try.'
(A legal separation – not
A *vinculo conjugii.*)

'O BAINES CAREW, my woe I've kept
A secret hitherto, you know;' –
(And BAINES CAREW, ESQUIRE, he wept
To hear that BAGG *had* any woe).

'My case, indeed, is passing sad.
My wife – whom I considered true –
With brutal conduct drives me mad.'
'I am appalled,' said BAINES CAREW.

'What! sound the matrimonial knell
Of worthy people such as these!
Why was I an attorney? Well –
Go on to the *saevitia*, please.'

'Domestic bliss has proved my bane, –
A harder case you never heard,
My wife (in other matters sane)
Pretends that I'm a Dicky Bird!

'She makes me sing, «Too-whit, too-wee!»
And stand upon a rounded stick,
And always introduces me
To every one as «Pretty Dick»!'

'Oh dear,' said weeping BAINES CAREW,
'This is the direst case I know.'
'I'm grieved,' said BAGG, 'at paining you –
To COBB and POLTERTHWAITE I'll go –

'To COBB's cold, calculating ear
My gruesome sorrows I'll impart' –
'No; stop,' said BAINES, 'I'll dry my tear,
And steel my sympathetic heart.'

'She makes me perch upon a tree,
Rewarding me with, «Sweety – nice!»
And threatens to exhibit me
With four or five performing mice.'

'Restrain my tears I wish I could'
(Said BAINES), 'I don't know what to do.'
Said CAPTAIN BAGG, 'You're very good.'
'Oh, not at all,' said BAINES CAREW.

'She makes me fire a gun,' said BAGG;
'And at a preconcerted word,
Climb up a ladder with a flag,
Like any street-performing bird.

'She places sugar in my way –
In public places calls me «Sweet!»
She gives me groundsel every day,
And hard canary-seed to eat.'

'Oh, woe! oh, sad! oh, dire to tell!'
(Said BAINES). 'Be good enough to stop.'
And senseless on the floor he fell
With unpremeditated flop!

Said CAPTAIN BAGG, 'Well, really I
   Am grieved to think it pains you so.
I thank you for your sympathy;
   But, hang it – come – I say, you know!'

But BAINES lay flat upon the floor,
   Convulsed with sympathetic sob; –
The Captain toddled off next door,
   And gave the case to MR COBB.

Thomas Winterbottom Hance

IN all the towns and cities fair
  On Merry England's broad expanse,
No swordsman ever could compare
  With THOMAS WINTERBOTTOM HANCE.

The dauntless lad could fairly hew
  A silken handkerchief in twain,
Divide a leg of mutton too –
  And this without unwholesome strain.

On whole half-sheep, with cunning trick,
  His sabre sometimes he'd employ –
No bar of lead, however thick,
  Had terrors for the stalwart boy.

At Dover daily he'd prepare
  To hew and slash, behind, before –
Which aggravated MONSIEUR PIERRE,
  Who watched him from the Calais shore.

It caused good PIERRE to swear and dance,
  The sight annoyed and vexed him so;
He was the bravest man in France –
  He said so, and he ought to know.

'Regardez, donc, ce cochon gros –
  Ce polisson! Oh, sacré bleu!
Son sabre, son plomb, et ses gigots!
  Comme cela m'ennuye, enfin, mon Dieu!

'Il sait que les foulards de soie
  Give no retaliating whack –
Les gigots morts n'ont pas de quoi –
  Le plomb don't ever hit you back.'

But every day the headstrong lad
  Cut lead and mutton more and more;
And every day poor PIERRE, half mad,
  Shrieked loud defiance from his shore.

HANCE had a mother, poor and old,
  A simple, harmless village dame,
Who crowed and clapped as people told
  Of WINTERBOTTOM's rising fame.

She said, 'I'll be upon the spot
  To see my TOMMY's sabre-play;'
And so she left her leafy cot,
And walked to Dover in a day.

PIERRE had a doting mother, who
  Had heard of his defiant rage:
His Ma was nearly eighty-two,
  And rather dressy for her age.

At HANCE's doings every morn,
  With sheer delight *his* mother cried;
And MONSIEUR PIERRE's contemptuous scorn
  Filled *his* mamma with proper pride.

But HANCE's powers began to fail –
  His constitution was not strong –
And PIERRE, who once was stout and hale,
  Grew thin from shouting all day long.

Their mothers saw them pale and wan,
  Maternal anguish tore each breast,
And so they met to find a plan
  To set their offsprings' minds at rest.

Said MRS HANCE, 'Of course I shrinks
  From bloodshed, ma'am, as you're aware,
But still they'd better meet, I thinks.'
  'Assurément!' said MADAME PIERRE.

A sunny spot in sunny France
  Was hit upon for this affair;
The ground was picked by MRS HANCE,
  The stakes were pitched by MADAME PIERRE.

Said MRS H., 'Your work you see –
Go in, my noble boy, and win.'
'En garde, mon fils!' said MADAME P.
'Allons!' 'Go on!' 'En garde!' 'Begin!'

(The mothers were of decent size,
Though not particularly tall;
But in the sketch that meets your eyes
I've been obliged to draw them small.)

Loud sneered the doughty man of France,
'Ho! ho! Ho! ho! Ha! ha! Ha! ha!'
'The French for «Pish!»' said THOMAS HANCE.
Said PIERRE, 'L'Anglais, Monsieur, pour «Bah!»'

Said Mrs H., 'Come, one! two! three! –
We're sittin' here to see all fair.'
'C'est magnifique!' said Madame P.,
'Mais, parbleu! ce n'est pas la guerre!'

'Je scorn un foe si lâche que vous,'
Said Pierre, the doughty son of France.
'I fight not coward foe like you!'
Said our undaunted Tommy Hance.

'The French for «Pooh!»' our Tommy cried.
'L'Anglais pour «Va!»' the Frenchman crowed.
And so, with undiminished pride,
Each went on his respective road.

A Discontented Sugar Broker

A GENTLEMAN of City fame
  Now claims your kind attention;
East India broking was his game,
  His name I shall not mention;
    No one of finely-pointed sense
    Would violate a confidence,
      And shall *I* go
      And do it? No!
  His name I shall not mention.

He had a trusty wife and true,
  And very cosy quarters,
A manager, a boy or two,
  Six clerks, and seven porters,

A broker must be doing well
(As any lunatic can tell)
Who can employ
An active boy,
Six clerks, and seven porters.

His knocker advertised no dun,
No losses made him sulky,
He had one sorrow – only one –
He was extremely bulky.
A man must be, I beg to state,
Exceptionally fortunate
Who owns his chief
And only grief
Is – being very bulky.

'This load,' he'd say, 'I cannot bear;
I'm nineteen stone or twenty!
Henceforward I'll go in for air
And exercise in plenty.'
Most people think that, should it come,
They can reduce a bulging tum
To measures fair
By taking air
And exercise in plenty.

In every weather, every day,
Dry, muddy, wet, or gritty,
He took to dancing all the way
From Brompton to the City.

You do not often get the chance
Of seeing sugar-brokers dance
From their abode
In Fulham Road
Through Brompton to the City.

He braved the gay and guileless laugh
Of children with their nusses,
The loud uneducated chaff
Of clerks on omnibuses.
Against all minor things that rack
A nicely balanced mind, I'll back
The noisy chaff
And ill-bred laugh
Of clerks on omnibuses.

His friends, who heard his money chink,
And saw the house he rented,
And knew his wife, could never think
What made him discontented.
It never entered their pure minds
That fads are of eccentric kinds,
Nor would they own
That fat alone
Could make one discontented.

'Your riches know no kind of pause,
Your trade is fast advancing;
You dance – but not for joy, because
You weep as you are dancing.
To dance implies that man is glad,
To weep implies that man is sad;
But here are you
Who do the two –
You weep as you are dancing!'

His mania soon got noised about
And into all the papers;
His size increased beyond a doubt
For all his reckless capers:
It may seem singular to you,
But all his friends admit it true –
The more he found
His figure round,
The more he cut his capers.

His bulk increased – no matter that –
He tried the more to toss it –
He never spoke of it as 'fat'
But 'adipose deposit'.
Upon my word, it seems to me
Unpardonable vanity
(And worse than that)
To call your fat
An 'adipose deposit'.

At length his brawny knees gave way,
And on the carpet sinking,
Upon his shapeless back he lay
And kicked away like winking.
Instead of seeing in his state
The finger of unswerving Fate,
He laboured still
To work his will,
And kicked away like winking.

His friends, disgusted with him now,
Away in silence wended –

I hardly like to tell you how
   This dreadful story ended.
      The shocking sequel to impart,
      I must employ the limner's art –
            If you would know,
            This sketch will show
   How his exertions ended.

MORAL

I hate to preach – I hate to prate –
   I'm no fanatic croaker,
But learn contentment from the fate
   Of this East India broker.
      He'd everything a man of taste
      Could ever want, except a waist:
            And discontent
            His size anent,
And bootless perseverance blind,
Completely wrecked the peace of mind
   Of this East India broker.

Ellen McJones Aberdeen

Macphairson Clonglocketty Angus McClan
Was the son of an elderly labouring man,
You've guessed him a Scotchman, shrewd reader, at sight,
And p'r'aps altogether, shrewd reader, you're right.

From the bonnie blue Forth to the hills of Deeside,
Round by Dingwall and Wrath to the mouth of the Clyde,
There wasn't a child or a woman or man
Who could pipe with Clonglocketty Angus McClan.

No other could wake such detestable groans,
With reed and with chaunter – with bag and with drones:
All day and all night he delighted the chiels
With sniggering pibrochs and jiggety reels.

He'd clamber a mountain and squat on the ground,
And the neighbouring maidens would gather around
To list to his pipes and to gaze in his een,
Especially ELLEN McJONES ABERDEEN.

All loved their McCLAN, save a Sassenach brute,
Who came to the Highlands to fish and to shoot;
He dressed himself up in a Highlander way,
Tho' his name it was PATTISON CORBY TORBAY.

TORBAY had incurred a good deal of expense
To make him a Scotchman in every sense;
But this is a matter, you'll readily own,
That isn't a question of tailors alone.

A Sassenach chief may be bonily built,
He may purchase a sporran, a bonnet, and kilt;
Stick a skean in his hose – wear an acre of stripes –
But he cannot assume an affection for pipes.

CLONGLOCKETTY's pipings all night and all day
Quite frenzied poor PATTISON CORBY TORBAY;
The girls were amused at his singular spleen,
Especially ELLEN McJONES ABERDEEN.

'Macphairson Clonglocketty Angus, my lad,
With pibrochs and reels you are driving me mad.
If you really must play on that cursed affair,
My goodness! play something resembling an air.'

Boiled over the blood of Macphairson McClan –
The Clan of Clonglocketty rose as one man;
For all were enraged at the insult, I ween –
Especially Ellen McJones Aberdeen.

'Let's show,' said McClan, 'to this Sassenach loon
That the bagpipes *can* play him a regular tune.
Let's see,' said McClan, as he thoughtfully sat,
'*In My Cottage* is easy – I'll practise at that.'

He blew at his 'Cottage', and blew with a will,
For a year, seven months, and a fortnight, until
(You'll hardly believe it) McClan, I declare,
Elicited something resembling an air.

It was wild – it was fitful – as wild as the breeze –
It wandered about into several keys;
It was jerky, spasmodic, and harsh, I'm aware,
But still it distinctly suggested an air.

The Sassenach screamed, and the Sassenach danced,
He shrieked in his agony – bellowed and pranced;
And the maidens who gathered rejoiced at the scene –
Especially Ellen McJones Aberdeen.

'Hech gather, hech gather, hech gather around;
And fill a' yer lugs wi' the exquisite sound.
An air fra' the bagpipes – beat that if ye can!
Hurrah for Clonglocketty Angus McClan!'

The fame of his piping spread over the land:
Respectable widows proposed for his hand,
And maidens came flocking to sit on the green –
Especially Ellen McJones Aberdeen.

One morning the fidgety Sassenach swore
He'd stand it no longer – he drew his claymore,
And (this was, I think, in extremely bad taste)
Divided Clonglocketty close to the waist.

Oh! loud were the wailings for Angus McClan –
Oh! deep was the grief for that excellent man;
The maids stood aghast at the horrible scene –
Especially Ellen McJones Aberdeen.

It sorrowed poor Pattison Corby Torbay
To find them 'take on' in this serious way;
He pitied the poor little fluttering birds,
And solaced their souls with the following words:

'Oh, maidens,' said Pattison, touching his hat,
'Don't snivel, my dears, for a fellow like that;
Observe, I'm a very superior man,
A much better fellow than Angus McClan.'

They smiled when he winked and addressed them as 'dears',
And they all of them vowed, as they dried up their tears,
A pleasanter gentleman never was seen –
Especially Ellen McJones Aberdeen.

Gentle Alice Brown

IT was a robber's daughter, and her name was ALICE BROWN,
Her father was the terror of a small Italian town;
Her mother was a foolish, weak, but amiable old thing;
But it isn't of her parents that I'm going for to sing.

As ALICE was a-sitting at her window-sill one day
A beautiful young gentleman he chanced to pass that way;
She cast her eyes upon him, and he looked so good and true,
That she thought, 'I could be happy with a gentleman like you!'

And every morning passed her house that cream of gentlemen,
She knew she might expect him at a quarter unto ten;
A sorter in the Custom-house, it was his daily road
(The Custom-house was fifteen minutes' walk from her abode).

But ALICE was a pious girl, who knew it wasn't wise
To look at strange young sorters with expressive purple eyes;
So she sought the village priest to whom her family confessed,
The priest by whom their little sins were carefully assessed.

'Oh, holy father,' ALICE said, ''twould grieve you, would it not,
To discover that I was a most disreputable lot?
Of all unhappy sinners I'm the most unhappy one!'
The padre said, 'Whatever have you been and gone and done?'

'I have helped mamma to steal a little kiddy from its dad,
I've assisted dear papa in cutting up a little lad,
I've planned a little burglary and forged a little cheque,
And slain a little baby for the coral on its neck!'

The worthy pastor heaved a sigh, and dropped a silent tear,
And said, 'You mustn't judge yourself too heavily, my dear:
It's wrong to murder babies, little corals for to fleece;
But sins like these one expiates at half-a-crown apiece.

'Girls will be girls – you're very young, and flighty in your
mind;
Old heads upon young shoulders we must not expect to
find:
We mustn't be too hard upon these little girlish tricks –
Let's see – five crimes at half-a-crown – exactly twelve-
and-six.'

'Oh, father,' little ALICE cried, 'your kindness makes me
weep,
You do these little things for me so singularly cheap –
Your thoughtful liberality I never can forget;
But oh! there is another crime I haven't mentioned yet!

'A pleasant-looking gentleman, with pretty purple eyes,
I've noticed at my window, as I've sat a-catching flies;
He passes by it every day as certain as can be –
I blush to say I've winked at him, and he has winked at me!'

'For shame,' said FATHER PAUL, 'my erring daughter!
On my word
This is the most distressing news that I have ever heard.
Why, naughty girl, your excellent papa has pledged your
hand
To a promising young robber, the lieutenant of his band!

'This dreadful piece of news will pain your worthy parents
so!
They are the most remunerative customers I know;

For many many years they've kept starvation from my
doors:
I never knew so criminal a family as yours!

'The common country folk in this insipid neighbourhood
Have nothing to confess, they're so ridiculously good;
And if you marry any one respectable at all,
Why, you'll reform, and what will then become of
FATHER PAUL?'

The worthy priest, he up and drew his cowl upon his crown,
And started off in haste to tell the news to ROBBER BROWN –
To tell him how his daughter, who was now for marriage fit,
Had winked upon a sorter, who reciprocated it.

Good ROBBER BROWN he muffled up his anger pretty
well:
He said 'I have a notion, and that notion I will tell;

I will nab this gay young sorter, terrify him into fits,
And get my gentle wife to chop him into little bits.

'I've studied human nature, and I know a thing or two:
Though a girl may fondly love a living gent, as many do –
A feeling of disgust upon her senses there will fall
When she looks upon his body chopped particularly small.'

He traced that gallant sorter to a still suburban square;
He watched his opportunity and seized him unaware;
He took a life-preserver and he hit him on the head,
And MRS BROWN dissected him before she went to bed.

And pretty little ALICE grew more settled in her mind,
She never more was guilty of a weakness of the kind,
Until at length good ROBBER BROWN bestowed her
pretty hand
On the promising young robber, the lieutenant of his band.

Annie Protheroe

A LEGEND OF STRATFORD-LE-BOW

OH! listen to the tale of little ANNIE PROTHEROE.
She kept a small post-office in the neighbourhood of Bow;
She loved a skilled mechanic, who was famous in his day –
A gentle executioner whose name was GILBERT CLAY.

I think I hear you say, 'A dreadful subject for your rhymes!'
O reader, do not shrink – he didn't live in modern times!
He lived so long ago (the sketch will show it at a glance)
That all his actions glitter with the limelight of Romance.

In busy times he laboured at his gentle craft all day –
'No doubt you mean his Cal-craft' you amusingly will say –
But, no – he didn't operate with common bits of string,
He was a Public Headsman, which is quite another thing.

And when his work was over, they would ramble o'er the
lea,
And sit beneath the frondage of an elderberry tree.
And ANNIE's simple prattle entertained him on his walk,
For public executions formed the subject of her talk.

And sometimes he'd explain to her, which charmed her
very much,
How famous operators vary very much in touch,
And then, perhaps, he'd show how he himself performed
the trick,
And illustrate his meaning with a poppy and a stick.

Or, if it rained, the little maid would stop at home, and
look
At his favourable notices, all pasted in a book,
And then her cheek would flush – her swimming eyes
would dance with joy
In a glow of admiration at the prowess of her boy.

One summer eve, at supper-time, the gentle GILBERT said
(As he helped his pretty ANNIE to a slice of collared head),
'This reminds me I must settle on the next ensuing day
The hash of that unmitigated villain PETER GRAY.'

He saw his ANNIE tremble and he saw his ANNIE start,
Her changing colour trumpeted the flutter at her heart;

Young GILBERT's manly bosom rose and sank with
jealous fear,
And he said, 'O gentle ANNIE, what's the meaning of this
here?'

And ANNIE answered, blushing in an interesting way,
'You think, no doubt, I'm sighing for that felon PETER
GRAY:
That I was his young woman is unquestionably true,
But not since I began a-keeping company with you.'

Then GILBERT, who was irritable, rose and loudly swore
He'd know the reason why if she refused to tell him more;
And she answered (all the woman in her flashing from her
eyes),
'You mustn't ask no questions, and you won't be told no
lies!

'Few lovers have the privilege enjoyed, my dear, by you,
Of chopping off a rival's head and quartering him too!

Of vengeance, dear, to-morrow you will surely take your
fill!'
And GILBERT ground his molars as he answered her, 'I
will!'

Young GILBERT rose from table with a stern determined
look,
And, frowning, took an inexpensive hatchet from its hook;
And ANNIE watched his movements with an interested
air –
For the morrow – for the morrow he was going to prepare!

He chipped it with a hammer and he chopped it with a bill,
He poured sulphuric acid on the edge of it, until
This terrible Avenger of the Majesty of Law
Was far less like a hatchet than a dissipated saw.

And ANNIE said, 'O GILBERT, dear, I do not understand
Why ever you are injuring that hatchet in your hand?'
He said, 'It is intended for to lacerate and flay
The neck of that unmitigated villain PETER GRAY!'

'Now, GILBERT,' ANNIE answered, 'wicked headsman,
just beware –
I won't have PETER tortured with that horrible affair;
If you appear with that, you may depend you'll rue the day.'
But GILBERT said, 'Oh, shall I?' which was just his nasty
way.

He saw a look of anger from her eyes distinctly dart,
For ANNIE was a woman, and had pity in her heart!
She wished him a good evening – he answered with a
glare;
She only said, 'Remember, for your ANNIE will be there!'

* * * * *

The morrow GILBERT boldly on the scaffold took his
stand,
With a vizor on his face and with a hatchet in his hand,
And all the people noticed that the Engine of the Law
Was far less like a hatchet than a dissipated saw.

The felon very coolly loosed his collar and his stock,
And placed his wicked head upon the handy little block.
The hatchet was uplifted for to settle PETER GRAY,
When GILBERT plainly heard a woman's voice exclaim-
ing, 'Stay!'

'Twas ANNIE, gentle ANNIE, as you'll easily believe.
'O GILBERT, you must spare him, for I bring him a re-
prieve,

It came from our Home Secretary many weeks ago,
And passed through that post-office which I used to keep
at Bow.

'I loved you, loved you madly, and you know it, GILBERT
CLAY,
And as I'd quite surrendered all idea of PETER GRAY,
I quietly suppressed it, as you'll clearly understand,
For I thought it might be awkward if he came and claimed
my hand.

'In anger at my secret (which I could not tell before)
To lacerate poor PETER GRAY vindictively you swore;
I told you if you used that blunted axe you'd rue the day,
And so you will, young GILBERT, for I'll marry PETER
GRAY!'

[*And so she did.*

Gregory Parable, LL.D.

A LEAFY cot, where no dry rot
Had ever been by tenant seen,
Where ivy clung and wopses stung,
Where beeses hummed and drummed and strummed,
Where treeses grew and breezes blew –
A thatchy roof, quite waterproof,
Where countless herds of dicky-birds
Built twiggy beds to lay their heads
(My mother begs I'll make it 'eggs,'
But though it's true that dickies do
Construct a nest with chirpy noise,
With view to rest their eggy joys,
'Neath eavy sheds, yet eggs and beds,
As I explain to her in vain
Five hundred times, are faulty rhymes).
'Neath such a cot, built on a plot
Of freehold land, dwelt MARY and
Her worthy father, named by me
GREGORY PARABLE, LL.D.

He knew no guile, this simple man,
No worldly wile, or plot, or plan,
Except that plot of freehold land
That held the cot, and MARY, and
Her worthy father, named by me
GREGORY PARABLE, LL.D.

A grave and learned scholar he,
Yet simple as a child could be.
He'd shirk his meal to sit and cram
A goodish deal of Eton Gram.
No man alive could him nonplus
With vocative of *filius*;

No man alive more fully knew
The passive of a verb or two;
None better knew the worth than he
Of words that end in *b*, *d*, *t*.
Upon his green in early spring
He might be seen endeavouring
To understand the hooks and crooks
Of HENRY and his Latin books,

Or calling for his 'Caesar on
The Gallic War,' like any don.
Or, p'raps, expounding unto all
How mythic Balbus built a wall.
So lived the sage who's named by me
Gregory Parable, ll.d.

To him one autumn day there came
A lovely youth of mystic name:
He took a lodging in the house,
And fell a-dodging snipe and grouse,
For, oh! that mild scholastic one
Let shooting for a single gun.

By three or four, when sport was o'er,
The Mystic One laid by his gun,
And made sheep's eyes of giant size,

Till after tea, at MARY P.
And MARY P. (so kind was she),
She, too, made eyes of giant size,
Whose every dart right through the heart
Appeared to run that Mystic One.
The Doctor's whim engrossing him,
He did not know they flirted so.
For, save at tea, '*musa musae*,'
As I'm advised, monopolized
And rendered blind his giant mind.
But looking up above his cup
One afternoon, he saw them spoon.
'Aha!' quoth he, 'you naughty lass!
As quaint old OVID says, «Amas!»'

The Mystic Youth avowed the truth,
And, claiming ruth, he said, 'In sooth
I love your daughter, aged man:
Refuse to join us if you can.
Treat not my offer, sir, with scorn,
I'm wealthy though I'm lowly born.'
'Young sir,' the aged scholar said,
'I never thought you meant to wed:
Engrossed completely with my books,
I little noticed lovers' looks.
I've lived so long away from man,
I do not know of any plan
By which to test a lover's worth,
Except, perhaps, the test of birth.

I've half forgotten in this wild
A father's duty to his child.
It is his place, I think it's said,
To see his daughters richly wed
To dignitaries of the earth,
If possible, of noble birth.
If noble birth is not at hand,
A father may, I understand
(And this affords a chance for you),
Be satisfied to wed her to
A BOUCICAULT or BARING – which
Means any one who's very rich.
Now, there's an Earl who lives hard by, –
My child and I will go and try
If he will make the maid his bride –
If not, to you she shall be tied.'

They sought the Earl that very day;
The Sage began to say his say.
The Earl (a very wicked man,
Whose face bore Vice's blackest ban)
Cut short the scholar's simple tale,
And said in voice to make them quail,
'Pooh! go along! you're drunk no doubt –
Here, PETERS, turn these people out!'

The Sage, rebuffed in mode uncouth,
Returning, met the Mystic Youth.
'My darling boy,' the Scholar said,
'Take MARY – blessings on your head!'

The Mystic Boy undid his vest,
And took a parchment from his breast,
And said, 'Now, by that noble brow,
I ne'er knew father such as thou!
The sterling rule of common sense
Now reaps its proper recompense.
Rejoice, my soul's unequalled Queen,
For I am Duke of Gretna Green!'

The Modest Couple

WHEN man and maiden meet, I like to see a drooping
eye,
I always droop my own – I am the shyest of the shy.
I'm also fond of bashfulness, and sitting down on thorns,
For modesty's a quality that womankind adorns.

Whenever I am introduced to any pretty maid,
My knees they knock together, just as if I were afraid;
I flutter, and I stammer, and I turn a pleasing red,
For to laugh, and flirt, and ogle I consider most ill-bred.

But still in all these matters, as in other things below,
There is a proper medium, as I'm about to show.
I do not recommend a newly-married pair to try
To carry on as PETER carried on with SARAH BLIGH.

Betrothed they were when very young – before they'd
learnt to speak
(For SARAH was but six days old, and PETER was a
week);
Though little more than babies at those early ages, yet
They bashfully would faint when they occasionally met.

They blushed, and flushed, and fainted, till they reached
the age of nine,
When PETER's good papa (he was a Baron of the Rhine)
Determined to endeavour some sound argument to find
To bring these shy young people to a proper frame of mind.

He told them that as SARAH was to be his PETER's bride,
They might at least consent to sit at table side by side;
He begged that they would now and then shake hands, till
he was hoarse,
Which SARAH thought indelicate, and PETER very coarse.

And PETER in a tremble to the blushing maid would say,
'You must excuse papa, MISS BLIGH, – it is his mountain
way.'
Says SARAH, 'His behaviour I'll endeavour to forget,
But your papa's the coarsest person that I ever met.

'He plighted us without our leave, when we were very
young,
Before we had begun articulating with the tongue.
His underbred suggestions fill your SARAH with alarm;
Why, gracious me! he'll ask us next to walk out arm-in-
arm!'

At length when SARAH reached the legal age of twenty-
one,
The Baron he determined to unite her to his son;
And SARAH in a fainting-fit for weeks unconscious lay,
And PETER blushed so hard you might have heard him
miles away.

And when the time arrived for taking SARAH to his heart,
They were married in two churches half-a-dozen miles
apart

(Intending to escape all public ridicule and chaff),
And the service was conducted by electric telegraph.

And when it was concluded, and the priest had said his say,
Until the time arrived when they were both to drive away,
They never spoke or offered for to fondle or to fawn,
For *he* waited in the attic, and *she* waited on the lawn.

At length, when four o'clock arrived, and it was time to go,
The carriage was announced, but decent SARAH answered
'No!
Upon my word, I'd rather sleep my everlasting nap,
Than go and ride alone with MR PETER in a trap.'

And PETER's over-sensitive and highly-polished mind
Wouldn't suffer him to sanction a proceeding of the kind;
And further, he declared he suffered overwhelming shocks
At the bare idea of having any coachman on the box.

So PETER in one chariot incontinently rushed,
While SARAH in a second trap sat modestly and blushed;
And MR NEWMAN'S coachman, on authority I've heard,
Drove away in gallant style upon the coach-box of a third.

Now, though this modest couple in the matter of the car
Were very likely carrying a principle too far,
I hold their shy behaviour was more laudable in them
Than that of PETER'S brother with MISS SARAH'S
sister EM.

ALPHONSO, who in cool assurance all creation licks,
He up and said to EMMIE (who had impudence for six),
'MISS EMILY, I love you – will you marry? Say the word!'
And EMILY said, 'Certainly, ALPHONSO, like a bird!'

I do not recommend a newly-married pair to try
To carry on as PETER carried on with SARAH BLIGH,
But still their shy behaviour was more laudable in them
Than that of PETER's brother with MISS SARAH's
sister EM.

Emily, John, James, and I

A DERBY LEGEND

EMILY JANE was a nursery maid,
  JAMES was a bold Life Guard,
And JOHN was a constable, poorly paid
  (And I am a doggerel bard).

A very good girl was EMILY JANE,
  JIMMY was good and true,
JOHN was a very good man in the main
  (And I am a good man too).

Rivals for EMMIE were JOHNNY and JAMES,
  Though EMILY liked them both;
She couldn't tell which had the strongest claims
  (And *I* couldn't take my oath).

But sooner or later you're certain to find
  Your sentiments can't lie hid –
JANE thought it was time that she made up her mind
  (And I think it was time she did).

Said JANE, with a smirk, and a blush on her face,
 'I'll promise to wed the boy
Who takes me to-morrow to Epsom Race!'
 (Which *I* would have done, with joy).

From JOHNNY escaped an expression of pain,
 But JIMMY said, 'Done with you!
I'll take you with pleasure, my EMILY JANE!'
 (And I would have said so too).

JOHN lay on the ground, and he roared like mad
 (For JOHNNY was sore perplexed),
And he kicked very hard at a very small lad
 (Which *I* often do, when vexed).

For JOHN was on duty next day with the Force,
 To punish all Epsom crimes;
Some people *will* cross, when they're clearing the course
 (I do it myself, sometimes).

* * * * *

The Derby Day sun glittered gaily on cads,
 On maidens with gamboge hair,
On sharpers and pickpockets, swindlers and pads
 (For I, with my harp, was there).

And JIMMY went down with his JANE that day,
 And JOHN by the collar or nape
Seized everybody who came in his way
 (And *I* had a narrow escape).

He noticed his EMILY JANE with JIM,
And envied the well-made elf;
And people remarked that he muttered 'Oh, dim!'
(I often say 'dim!' myself).

JOHN dogged them all day, without asking their leaves;
For his sergeant he told, aside,
That JIMMY and JANE were notorious thieves
(And I think he was justified).

But JAMES wouldn't dream of abstracting a fork,
And JENNY would blush with shame
At stealing so much as a bottle or cork
(A bottle I think fair game).

But, ah! there's another more serious crime!
They wickedly strayed upon
The course, at a critical moment of time
(I pointed them out to JOHN).

The constable fell on the pair in a crack –
And then, with a demon smile,
Let JENNY cross over, but sent JIMMY back
(I played on my harp the while).

Stern JOHNNY their agony loud derides
With a very triumphant sneer –
They weep and they wail from the opposite sides
(And *I* shed a silent tear).

And JENNY is crying away like mad,
And JIMMY is swearing hard;
And JOHNNY is looking uncommonly glad
(And I am a doggerel bard).

But JIMMY he ventured on crossing again
The scenes of our Isthmian Games –
JOHN caught him, and collared him, giving him pain
(I felt very much for JAMES).

JOHN led him away with a victor's hand,
And JIMMY was shortly seen
In the station-house under the grand Grand Stand
(As many a time *I've* been).

And JIMMY, bad boy, was imprisoned for life,
Though EMILY pleaded hard;
And JOHNNY had EMILY JANE to wife
(And I am a doggerel bard).

Hongree and Mabry

A RECOLLECTION OF A SURREY MELODRAMA

THE sun was setting in its wonted west,
When HONGREE, Sub-Lieutenant of Chassoores,
Met MAHRY DAUBIGNY, the Village Rose,
Under the Wizard's Oak – old trysting-place
Of those who loved in rosy Aquitaine.

They thought themselves unwatched, but they were not;
For HONGREE, Sub-Lieutenant of Chassoores,
Found in LIEUTENANT-COLONEL JOOLES DUBOSC
A rival, envious and unscrupulous,
Who thought it not foul scorn to dog his steps,
And listen, unperceived, to all that passed
Between the simple little Village Rose
And HONGREE, Sub-Lieutenant of Chassoores.

A clumsy barrack-bully was DUBOSC,
Quite unfamiliar with the well-bred tact
That actuates a proper gentleman
In dealing with a girl of humble rank.
You'll understand his coarseness when I say
He would have married MAHRY DAUBIGNY,
And dragged the unsophisticated girl
Into the whirl of fashionable life,
For which her singularly rustic ways,
Her breeding (moral, but extremely rude),
Her language (chaste, but ungrammatical),
Would absolutely have unfitted her.
How different to this unreflecting boor
Was HONGREE, Sub-Lieutenant of Chassoores!

Contemporary with the incident
Related in our opening paragraph,
Was that sad war 'twixt Gallia and ourselves
That followed on the treaty signed at Troyes;
And so LIEUTENANT-COLONEL JOOLES DUBOSC
(Brave soldier, he, with all his faults of style)
And HONGREE, Sub-Lieutenant of Chassoores,
Were sent by CHARLES of France against the lines
Of our Sixth HENRY (Fourteen twenty-nine),
To drive his legions out of Aquitaine.

When HONGREE, Sub-Lieutenant of Chassoores,
Returned (suspecting nothing) to his camp,
After his meeting with the Village Rose,

He found inside his barrack letter-box
A note from the commanding-officer,
Requiring his attendance at headquarters.
He went, and found LIEUTENANT-COLONEL JOOLES.

'Young HONGREE, Sub-Lieutenant of Chassoores,
This night we shall attack the English camp:
Be the «forlorn hope» yours – you'll lead it, sir,
And lead it too with credit, I've no doubt.
As every soul must certainly be killed
(For you are twenty 'gainst two thousand men),
It is not likely that you will return.
But what of that? you'll have the benefit
Of knowing that you die a soldier's death.'

Obedience was young HONGREE's strongest point,
But he imagined that he only owed
Allegiance to his MAHRY and his King.
'If MAHRY bade me lead these fated men,
I'd lead them – but I do not think she would.
If CHARLES, my King, said, «Go, my son, and die,»
I'd go, of course – my duty would be clear.
But MAHRY is in bed asleep, I hope,
And CHARLES, my King, a hundred leagues from this.
As for LIEUTENANT-COLONEL JOOLES DUBOSC,
How know I that our monarch would approve
The order he has given me to-night?
My King I've sworn in all things to obey –
I'll only take my orders from my King!'
Thus HONGREE, Sub-Lieutenant of Chassoores,
Interpreted the terms of his commission.

And HONGREE, who was wise as he was good,
Disguised himself that night in ample cloak,
Round flapping hat, and visor mask of black,
And made, unnoticed, for the English camp.
He passed the unsuspecting sentinels
(Who little thought a man in this disguise
Could be a proper object of suspicion),
And ere the curfew-bell had boomed 'lights out',
He found in audience Bedford's haughty Duke.

'Your Grace,' he said, 'start not – be not alarmed,
Although a Frenchman stands before your eyes.

I'm Hongree, Sub-Lieutenant of Chassoores.
My colonel will attack your camp to-night,
And orders me to lead the hope forlorn.
Now I am sure our excellent King Charles
Would not approve of this; but he 's away
A hundred leagues, and rather more than that.
So, utterly devoted to my King,
Blinded by my attachment to the throne,
And having but its interest at heart,
I feel it is my duty to disclose
All schemes that emanate from Colonel Jooles,
If I believe that they are not the kind
Of schemes that our good monarch could approve.'

'But how,' said Bedford's Duke, 'do you propose
That we should overthrow your colonel's scheme?'
And Hongree, Sub-Lieutenant of Chassoores,

Replied at once with never-failing tact:
'Oh sir, I know this cursed country well.
Entrust yourself and all your host to me;
I'll lead you safely by a secret path
Into the heart of COLONEL JOOLES' array,
And you can then attack them unprepared,
And slay my fellow-countrymen unarmed.'

The thing was done. The DUKE OF BEDFORD gave
The order, and two thousand fighting-men
Crept silently into the Gallic camp,
And slew the Frenchmen as they lay asleep;
And Bedford's haughty Duke slew COLONEL JOOLES,
And married MAHRY, pride of Aquitaine,
To HONGREE, Sub-Lieutenant of Chassoores.

Etiquette

THE *Ballyshannon* foundered off the coast of Cariboo,
And down in fathoms many went the captain and the crew;
Down went the owners – greedy men whom hope of gain allured:
Oh, dry the starting tear, for they were heavily insured.

Besides the captain and the mate, the owners and the crew,
The passengers were also drowned excepting only two:
Young PETER GRAY, who tasted teas for BAKER, CROOP, AND CO.,
And SOMERS, who from Eastern shores imported indigo.

These passengers, by reason of their clinging to a mast,
Upon a desert island were eventually cast.
They hunted for their meals, as ALEXANDER SELKIRK used,
But they couldn't chat together – they had not been introduced.

For PETER GRAY, and SOMERS too, though certainly in
trade,
Were properly particular about the friends they made;
And somehow thus they settled it without a word of
mouth –
That GRAY should take the northern half, while SOMERS
took the south.

On PETER's portion oysters grew – a delicacy rare,
But oysters were a delicacy PETER couldn't bear.
On SOMERS' side was turtle, on the shingle lying thick,
Which SOMERS couldn't eat, because it always made him
sick.

GRAY gnashed his teeth with envy as he saw a mighty store
Of turtle unmolested on his fellow-creature's shore:
The oysters at his feet aside impatiently he shoved,
For turtle, and his mother, were the only things he loved.

And SOMERS sighed in sorrow as he settled in the south,
For the thought of PETER's oysters brought the water to
his mouth.
He longed to lay him down upon the shelly bed, and stuff:
He had often eaten oysters, but had never had enough.

How they wished an introduction to each other they had had
When on board the *Ballyshannon*! And it drove them nearly
mad
To think how very friendly with each other they might get,
If it wasn't for the arbitrary rule of etiquette!

One day, when out a-hunting for the *mus ridiculus*,
GRAY overheard his fellow-man soliloquizing thus:
'I wonder how the playmates of my youth are getting on,
M'CONNELL, S. B. WALTERS, PADDY BYLES, and ROBINSON?'

These simple words made PETER as delighted as could be,
Old chummies at the Charterhouse were ROBINSON and he!
He walked straight up to SOMERS, then he turned extremely red,
Hesitated, hummed and hawed a bit, then cleared his throat, and said:

'I beg your pardon – pray forgive me if I seem too bold,
But you have breathed a name I knew familiarly of old.
You spoke aloud of ROBINSON – I happened to be by –
You know him?' 'Yes, extremely well.' 'Allow me – so
do I.'

It was enough: they felt they could more pleasantly get on,
For (ah, the magic of the fact!) they each knew
ROBINSON!
And MR SOMERS' turtle was at PETER's service quite,
And MR SOMERS punished PETER's oyster-beds all night.

They soon became like brothers from community of
wrongs:
They wrote each other little odes and sang each other
songs;
They told each other anecdotes disparaging their wives;
On several occasions, too, they saved each other's lives.

They felt quite melancholy when they parted for the night,
And got up in the morning soon as ever it was light;

Each other's pleasant company they reckoned so upon,
And all because it happened that they both knew
Robinson!

They lived for many years on that inhospitable shore,
And day by day they learned to love each other more and
more.
At last, to their astonishment, on getting up one day,
They saw a frigate anchored in the offing of the bay.

To Peter an idea occurred. 'Suppose we cross the main?
So good an opportunity may not occur again.'
And Somers thought a minute, then ejaculated, 'Done!
I wonder how my business in the City's getting on?'

'But stay,' said MR PETER: 'when in England, as you know,
I earned a living tasting teas for BAKER, CROOP, AND CO.,
I may be superseded – my employers think me dead!'
'Then come with me,' said SOMERS, 'and taste indigo instead.'

But all their plans were scattered in a moment when they found
The vessel was a convict ship from Portland, outward bound;
When a boat came off to fetch them, though they felt it very kind,
To go on board they firmly but respectfully declined.

As both the happy settlers roared with laughter at the joke,
They recognized a gentlemanly fellow pulling stroke:
'Twas ROBINSON – a convict, in an unbecoming frock!
Condemned to seven years for misappropriating stock!!!

They laughed no more, for SOMERS thought he had been rather rash
In knowing one whose friend had misappropriated cash;
And PETER thought a foolish tack he must have gone upon
In making the acquaintance of a friend of ROBINSON.

At first they didn't quarrel very openly, I've heard;
They nodded when they met, and now and then exchanged a word:
The word grew rare, and rarer still the nodding of the head,
And when they meet each other now, they cut each other dead.

To allocate the island they agreed by word of mouth,
And PETER takes the north again, and SOMERS takes the south;
And PETER has the oysters, which he hates, in layers thick,
And SOMERS has the turtle – turtle always makes him sick.

APPENDIX

A Note on Gilbert as Illustrator

BY PHILIP JAMES

THE first edition of *The Bab Ballads* is one of the brightest stars in the galaxy of the illustrated books which appeared in the sixties; although it is often overlooked by historians of book-illustration and although its author and illustrator, combined in the robust personality of W. S. Gilbert, is not mentioned in Forrest Reid's standard work on the illustrations of this decade. The wood-engravings have a wit and a punch – one might almost say a savagery – recalling many of Tenniel's designs for *Alice*, which in fact appeared in 1865, four years after Gilbert first started his contributions to the comic journal *Fun* and four years before these illustrated poems were first issued in book form as *The Bab Ballads*. One cannot resist the conclusion that the essential quality of the illustrations and their marked affinity were due in no small degree to the fact that the blocks for both books were engraved by the Dalziels.

In 1873 there appeared *More Bab Ballads* and in 1877 *Fifty Bab Ballads* which was a condensation of the two previous volumes. In his preface to the latter Gilbert wrote: 'The period during which they were written extended over some three or four years; many, however, were composed hastily, and under the discomforting necessity of having to turn out a quantity of lively verse by a certain day in every week. As it seemed to me (and to others) that the volumes were disfigured by the presence of these hastily written impostors, I thought it better to withdraw from both volumes such Ballads as seemed to show evidence of carelessness or undue haste. . . .'

In 1898 another, greatly enlarged, edition of *The Bab Ballads* was issued. This contained *Songs of a Savoyard* from the operas and about 200 new illustrations. Some seventy of the original cuts were either omitted or completely changed and the whole impression is one of unfortunate emasculation. The vigour had gone. This is, of course, largely due to the fact that the method of reproduction was by then the line-block with its faithful imitation of the fine pen stroke, instead of the wood-engraving with its heavy blacks and strong contrasts. By way of explanation one might suppose that Gilbert preferred to see his own drawings reproduced more or less in facsimile, instead of subjected to interpretation by a professional engraver. In his preface, already quoted on page 10 of this book, he justifies the alteration with the words: 'I have always felt that many of the original illustrations to *The Bab Ballads* erred gravely in the direction of unnecessary extravagance.' But, as Sir Max Beerbohm so aptly observed, 'so did *The Bab Ballads*! That is why the first drawings were so exactly right for them. To make these new drawings equally right, Mr Gilbert ought to have rewritten the poems. I am glad that his innate love for logic did not drive him to this double vandalism.'*

The extent of the vandalism was probably not so great as is implied and it would have been interesting to see whether in fact his original designs for the first edition did differ essentially in character from those for the second, of which 197 are now preserved in the Print Room at the British Museum. But, if they ever had existed on paper, they would probably have been destroyed, as so often happened, by the engravers when they transferred them to the block. It is almost certain, however, that Gilbert drew direct on to the block. This is confirmed by another statement by Max who, writing again of *The Bab Ballads*, mentions 'a sombre little quadrangle' in Clement's Inn, 'one of whose windows was pointed out to me as the window of the room in which Gilbert had written those poems and had cut the wood blocks that immortally illustrate them.'† The suggestion that Gilbert himself cut the blocks is a slip of the pen. The fact that he drew them on the block is, how-

* *Saturday Review*, 27 May 1905.
† Ibid., 14 May 1904.

ever, confirmed by a letter which he wrote to his publisher* reporting a dispute with Dalziels about the ownership of the blocks. In this he says: 'Perhaps it would be as well to draw the blocks again and return the originals to the Dalziels? I could improve considerably on the original sketches.' This was written in April 1882, when the pastoral and fairy magic of *Iolanthe* were taking shape. So the desire to water down his early fantasy was no sudden decision. Indeed the inclusion in the first edition of quite a large number of tame, insipid cuts, which it would seem the engraver was content to copy more or less slavishly rather than interpret with a strong mixture of artistic licence – and these were invariably the ones which were allowed to reappear in the edition of 1898 – suggests that the 'extravagance' was the engraver's rather than the artist's and that in Gilbert's character sentiment shared equally with satire.

* Mr Colin Franklin kindly searched the records of his firm, Routledge & Kegan Paul Ltd, and gave me permission to quote this letter.

I. BAINES CAREW, GENTLEMAN

11a. THOMAS WINTERBOTTOM HANCE

11b. THOMAS WINTERBOTTOM HANCE

IIC. THOMAS WINTERBOTTOM HANCE

11d. THOMAS WINTERBOTTOM HANCE

IIIa. ELLEN MCJONES ABERDEEN

111b. ELLEN MCJONES ABERDEEN

IIIC. ELLEN McJONES ABERDEEN

IVa. GENTLE ALICE BROWN

IVb. GENTLE ALICE BROWN

IVC. GENTLE ALICE BROWN

Of this book
one thousand five hundred copies
were printed and bound for Sir Allen Lane
at the University Press, Oxford.
The collotype plates were printed by the
Ganymed Press, London.
The type is Monotype Bell and the paper
Grosvenor Chater's Abbey Mills.
The line engravings were made by
John Swain and Son,
Barnet.